SUMMARY OF RELEASING THE ANOINTING

Walking in the Dynamic Flow of the Holy Spirit's Power

JAMES TAN

Copyright 2024–Harrison House

All rights reserved. This book is protected by the copyright laws of the United States of America. This book may not be copied or reprinted for commercial gain or profit. The use of short quotations or occasional page copying for personal or group study is permitted and encouraged. Permission will be granted upon request. Unless otherwise indicated, all scripture quotations are taken from the *King James Version* of the Bible. Used by permission. All rights reserved.

All emphasis within Scripture quotations is the author's own. Please note that Harrison House's publishing style capitalizes certain pronouns in Scripture that refer to the Father, Son, and Holy Spirit, and may differ from some publishers' styles. Take note that the name satan and related names are not capitalized. We choose not to acknowledge him, even to the point of violating grammatical rules.

Harrison House P.O. Box 310, Shippensburg, PA 17257-0310

This book and all other Harrison House's books are available at Christian bookstores and distributors worldwide.

For Worldwide Distribution.

Reach us on the Internet: www.harrisonhouse.com.

ISBN 13 TP: 9781667510163

ISBN 13 eBook: 9781667510170

CONTENTS

Introduction   v

1. Anointed to Know the Anointing   1
2. A Knowing Anointing   5
3. The Anointing Teaches Us   9
4. Anointed for Life   13
5. Salt and Light   17
6. Baptized in Fire   21
7. Our Progression in the Anointing   25
8. Reverence and Obedience: Keys to the Tangible Anointing   29
9. Jesus Builds His Church   33
10. Assorted Anointings on Assignment   37
11. The Foundation of the Apostles and Prophets   40
12. The Greater Anointing   44

About the Publisher   49

INTRODUCTION

❦

The anointing is a multifaceted manifestation of God's power, a spiritual endowment that transforms believers and empowers them to fulfill divine purposes. In the study of this divine empowerment, "Releasing the Anointing" explores the intricate ways in which the anointing operates within the life of a believer, providing a deeper understanding and practical guidance on how to activate and cultivate this spiritual phenomenon in one's life and community.

The concept of the anointing, rooted deeply in biblical doctrine, is often shrouded in mystery and relegated to the realms of the abstract. However, this book demystifies the anointing, making it accessible and actionable for every believer who seeks to walk in the footsteps of Jesus Christ. From the individual's personal spiritual growth to their impact on the church and society, the anointing is presented not just as a gift, but as a divine imperative for the Christian life.

INTRODUCTION

Throughout the chapters, readers will discover the different aspects of the anointing—from the individual anointing that heals, delivers, and sanctifies, to the corporate anointing that unites and empowers communities for spiritual warfare and worship. The book also delves into the historical and contemporary implications of the anointing, exploring how it has shaped church movements and individual lives across ages.

"Releasing the Anointing" serves as both a theological treatise and a practical handbook, offering biblical insights, historical perspectives, and contemporary applications. It challenges believers to not only seek the anointing but to actively engage in releasing it within their spheres of influence. Through scriptural exegesis, personal testimonies, and prophetic insights, this book aims to equip the reader with the knowledge and spiritual tools necessary to walk in the fullness of God's power.

As we embark on this exploration, we invite readers to open their hearts and minds to the transformative possibilities of the anointing. It is our prayer that this journey will not only enlighten but also ignite a fresh passion for deeper spiritual engagement and a more effective Christian witness in the world today. Let us step into the flow of the Spirit, releasing the anointing in ways that renew our lives, our churches, and our communities, bringing glory to God and advancing His kingdom on Earth.

CHAPTER 1

ANOINTED TO KNOW THE ANOINTING

Bible Verse

"Do you not know that you are the temple of God and that the Spirit of God dwells in you?" — 1 Corinthians 3:16

Introduction

This chapter delves into the distinctive roles and manifestations of the Holy Spirit across the Old and New Testaments, highlighting the transition from a temporary anointing for specific roles to an enduring presence within all believers. It explores the profound impact of this permanent indwelling, emphasizing the empowerment it provides to live a holy life and serve effectively in God's kingdom.

Word of Wisdom

"The Holy Spirit empowers us to live holy lives!" James Tan

. . .

Main Theme

The main theme of this chapter is the transformation of the Holy Spirit's role from a temporary external force in the Old Testament to a permanent indwelling presence in New Testament believers, enabling them to carry out God's will more fully and profoundly.

Key Points

- In the Old Testament, the Holy Spirit temporarily anointed prophets, kings, and priests, lifting once their specific tasks were completed.
- Under the New Covenant, believers are marked as permanent dwellings of the Holy Spirit, reflecting a superior covenant through the sacrifice of Jesus.
- The anointing in believers today empowers and consecrates them as part of a royal priesthood and a holy nation.
- The Holy Spirit's indwelling is meant to empower believers not just for service but for sanctification and personal transformation.
- Despite sin, the New Testament teaches that the Holy Spirit does not depart from believers but rather, their receptivity to His guidance diminishes.
- The anointing is crucial for both public ministry and personal spiritual growth, highlighting the necessity of balance

between serving others and nurturing one's own spiritual life.

Key Themes

- **The Shift in the Holy Spirit's Role:** Unlike the temporary anointing of the Old Testament, the New Testament ushers in a permanent indwelling of the Holy Spirit in believers, fundamentally changing how they interact with God and fulfill His purposes.
- **Anointing as a Mark of Consecration:** The anointing sets believers apart, consecrating them as God's holy assembly. This sacred anointing enables believers to carry the presence of God, transforming them into agents of divine influence.
- **Empowerment through the Holy Spirit:** The chapter emphasizes that the anointing of the Holy Spirit is essential for overcoming sin and for spiritual growth, enabling believers to lead lives that are pleasing to God.
- **Ministry and Personal Growth:** The Holy Spirit equips believers with gifts suited for various forms of service within the church, while also nurturing their personal spiritual development, demonstrating that effective ministry flows from a vibrant personal relationship with God.
- **The Permanence of the Holy Spirit's Presence:** Despite the challenges of sin, the Holy Spirit remains with believers, guiding and sanctifying them, which is a

testament to God's faithfulness and the superior covenant of the New Testament.

Conclusion

"Anointed to Know the Anointing" compellingly outlines the evolution of the Holy Spirit's role from a temporary external influence to a permanent internal presence within believers. This shift not only enhances the believer's capacity for service but also deepens their personal relationship with God, ensuring their growth and effectiveness in fulfilling His divine purposes. The chapter encourages believers to embrace this anointing, which is integral to living out the fullness of their Christian faith.

CHAPTER 2

A KNOWING ANOINTING

Bible Verse

"But you have an anointing from the Holy One, and you know all things." — 1 John 2:20

Introduction

This chapter explores the multifaceted nature of the anointing by the Holy Spirit, emphasizing its role beyond emotional experiences to include guidance, instruction, and empowerment in both spiritual and practical aspects of life. It delves into how the anointing functions similarly across different roles and individuals, providing wisdom and capabilities according to God's purposes.

Word of Wisdom

"The anointing within does not guide loudly, but it does guide clearly!" James Tan

Main Theme

The main theme of this chapter is the comprehensive and guiding role of the anointing in the believer's life, which encompasses not just spiritual empowerment but also practical guidance in daily activities and decisions.

Key Points

- The anointing from the Holy Spirit is singular but manifests in diverse ways across different contexts and individuals.
- The Holy Spirit equips individuals with specific anointings that align with their God-given roles and tasks, enhancing their effectiveness in both spiritual and secular fields.
- Not just for traditional ministry roles, the anointing extends to all believers, empowering them in their specific fields, like craftsmanship.
- The anointing provides believers with an internal guide, enhancing discernment and decision-making in both big and small life choices.
- Believers are equipped with an anointing that helps discern the spiritual root of issues, not just their outward manifestations.
- The anointing is accessible and active in every believer, providing a constant source of guidance and empowerment.

Key Themes

- **Multifunctional Nature of the Anointing:** The anointing is not restricted to creating spiritual experiences but is a practical guide in daily life, equipping believers with the necessary skills and wisdom for their specific tasks and challenges.
- **Universal Access to the Anointing:** Unlike the Old Testament where the anointing was limited to specific individuals, in the New Covenant, the anointing is available to all believers, enhancing their capabilities in a wide range of endeavors.
- **Guidance in Decision-Making:** The anointing acts as an internal compass that guides believers away from potential harm and toward God's purposes, helping them make decisions that align with divine wisdom.
- **Discernment of Spiritual Matters:** Through the anointing, believers can discern the spiritual forces at work in various situations, enabling them to address these issues with spiritual authority and insight.
- **Empowerment for All Believers:** The anointing empowers every believer, not just those in overtly spiritual roles, indicating that God values and uses the contributions of all His followers in diverse fields.

Conclusion

"A Knowing Anointing" emphasizes the extensive and versatile role of the Holy Spirit's anointing in a believer's life, which transcends traditional spiritual roles to include guidance and empowerment in everyday affairs. This chapter reassures believers of the continuous presence and assistance of the Holy Spirit, encouraging them to rely on this divine anointing for wisdom, protection, and empowerment in fulfilling their God-given purposes.

CHAPTER 3

THE ANOINTING TEACHES US

Bible Verse

"But the Helper, the Holy Spirit, whom the Father will send in My name, He will teach you all things, and bring to your remembrance all things that I said to you." — John 14:26

Introduction

This chapter explores how the anointing by the Holy Spirit serves as a divine instructor for believers, guiding them in both spiritual growth and practical life applications. It details the ways in which the anointing not only empowers but also educates, ensuring believers are both knowledgeable in the Word of God and adept in applying it to their lives.

Word of Wisdom

"The anointing within does not guide loudly, but it does guide clearly!" James Tan

Main Theme

The main theme of this chapter is the educational role of the anointing in the life of a believer, illustrating how the Holy Spirit teaches through remembrance, illumination, direct revelation, and through ordained teachers within the Body of Christ.

Key Points

- The Holy Spirit's anointing teaches believers by reminding them of God's Word and enlightening them to its application.
- The anointing illuminates spiritual truths, providing deeper insights into Scripture and God's will.
- It empowers believers to recall and articulate biblical truths accurately and relevantly, particularly in ministry settings.
- The anointing enables personal revelations that align with God's Word, guiding believers in their daily lives.
- The Holy Spirit uses people within the five-fold ministry to further impart spiritual knowledge and understanding.
- Direct communication from the Holy Spirit complements and enhances the lessons learned from human teachers.

Key Themes

- **Interactive and Responsive Teaching:** The Holy Spirit actively interacts with believers by bringing biblical truths to mind and applying these truths to current situations. This responsive teaching mechanism ensures that the spiritual lessons are not only learned but are also relevant and timely.

- **Comprehensive Spiritual Illumination:** Through the anointing, believers receive a deeper understanding of Scripture. This illumination goes beyond intellectual comprehension, embedding divine truths in the believer's heart and mind, which influences their actions and decisions.
- **Dynamic Learning Process:** The anointing facilitates a dynamic learning process where believers are taught both through personal study and communal teaching. This ensures a well-rounded spiritual education that is both self-driven and community-supported.
- **Provision of Direct Revelation:** The anointing provides direct revelations to believers, which are not new doctrines but deeper insights into existing truths, helping believers navigate complex life situations with divine wisdom.
- **Empowerment for Articulation:** Besides learning, the anointing empowers believers to articulate their faith effectively. This is crucial for personal ministry and for fulfilling the Great Commission, as believers can confidently and accurately share the gospel.

Conclusion

"The Anointing Teaches Us" reveals the multifaceted ways in which the Holy Spirit educates believers, ensuring they are not only hearers of the Word but also doers. Through remembrance, illumination, direct revelation, and the ministry of others, the anointing nurtures a deep and active understanding of the faith, equipping believers to live out their divine purpose with wisdom and integrity. This chapter encourages believers to lean into the teaching aspect of the anointing, cultivating a receptive heart that is continually shaped by the truths of Scripture.

CHAPTER 4

ANOINTED FOR LIFE

Bible Verse

"No temptation has overtaken you except such as is common to man; but God is faithful, who will not allow you to be tempted beyond what you are able, but with the temptation will also make the way of escape, that you may be able to bear it." — 1 Corinthians 10:13

Introduction

This chapter explores the pervasive role of the Holy Spirit's anointing in everyday life, emphasizing that our journey with God begins here on earth and prepares us for eternal life. It highlights the necessity of allowing the Holy Spirit to lead, illustrating that the anointing is not just for emergencies but is essential for daily victories and growth.

Word of Wisdom

"God in His mercy only allows progressive giants!" James Tan

Main Theme

The main theme of this chapter is the constant and daily necessity of the Holy Spirit's anointing in the believer's life, which empowers, teaches, and guides us in our daily activities and spiritual growth, preparing us for larger challenges.

Key Points

- The anointing of the Holy Spirit is essential for daily living, not just for crises.
- True discipleship involves following the Holy Spirit's lead in everyday matters.
- The Holy Spirit's guidance prepares believers for future challenges, much like David was prepared for Goliath.
- Regular, mundane activities are training grounds for spiritual growth and future victories.
- The anointing teaches us privately first, ensuring we are ready for public ministry and challenges.
- Obedience to the Holy Spirit's promptings is crucial; it is more significant than sacrifices.

Key Themes

- **Training for Spiritual Battles:** The chapter explains that just as David was prepared by God through smaller battles with lions and bears before facing Goliath, believers are similarly prepared through daily obedience and small victories. This preparation is crucial for facing larger spiritual challenges successfully.
- **Continuous Anointing:** It stresses the importance of recognizing and cooperating with the Holy Spirit's anointing every day, not just during times of need. This daily cooperation with the Holy Spirit ensures a continual growth and readiness for any spiritual warfare or tasks.
- **Importance of Private Growth:** Before public victories, there is often private obedience and growth. The chapter underlines the necessity of being faithful in private responsibilities, which equips us with the grace and anointing needed for public and larger roles.
- **The Holy Spirit as a Teacher:** The anointing teaches us gradually and gently, preparing us incrementally for bigger roles and challenges. This teaching is fundamental for developing a deep, mature Christian life that can withstand and overcome significant trials.
- **Obedience Over Sacrifice:** Emphasizes the importance of immediate obedience to the Holy Spirit's promptings over later sacrifices. Immediate obedience allows believers to operate under God's grace and

anointing, making what might seem like sacrifices at the moment into opportunities for divine grace and victory.

Conclusion

"Anointed for Life" reinforces the essential role of the Holy Spirit's anointing in everyday life, guiding believers from small victories to significant triumphs. The chapter encourages believers to embrace the daily guidance of the Holy Spirit, ensuring that each step taken is anointed and directed towards God's will, building up to a life that not only anticipates but actively participates in God's eternal kingdom. The anointing isn't just for extraordinary moments; it is crucial for the full spectrum of the believer's life, embodying the principle that we are trained and equipped for every good work through the Spirit's power and guidance.

CHAPTER 5

SALT AND LIGHT

Bible Verse

"You are the salt of the earth. ...You are the light of the world. A city that is set on a hill cannot be hidden. ...Let your light so shine before men, that they may see your good works and glorify your Father in heaven." — Matthew 5:13-14,16

Introduction

This chapter focuses on the transformative and pervasive power of the anointing in a believer's life, illustrating how God uses us to manifest His presence and work in the world, distinguishing the Church from any other organization through the unique power of the Holy Spirit.

Word of Wisdom

"The supply of the Spirit is only available on the paths of the Spirit!"
James Tan

Main Theme

The chapter delves into the purpose and impact of the anointing in the believer's life, emphasizing its role in guiding, empowering, and using Christians to carry out God's work on Earth, thereby making them effective agents of His will.

Key Points

- The anointing empowers believers to perform works that glorify God and distinguish them from secular efforts.
- To be sent by God means to move under His command, with His anointing accompanying and empowering the believer.
- The Holy Spirit guides the believer into paths that fulfill God's purposes, not personal desires.
- Being anointed involves carrying God's presence and power into every environment and situation.
- True anointing involves action, not just feelings or emotional experiences.
- The anointing teaches and leads believers in their specific callings, ensuring they operate within God's will.

Key Themes

- **Empowered to Influence:** The anointing enables believers to impact those

around them by living out the truths and power of the gospel. It's not merely for personal emotional experiences but for actionable, visible influence in the community and the world.
- **Distinctive Role of the Church:** Unlike other organizations that provide humanitarian aid, the Church's unique role is to bring spiritual freedom and healing through the anointing, which alone can truly set captives free from the deepest forms of bondage.
- **Obedience and Direction:** The anointing follows divine direction and obedience, not personal ambition. Believers are reminded that being 'sent' involves receiving and responding to God's specific commands, which is accompanied by His power and presence.
- **Sustained by the Spirit:** The Holy Spirit not only initiates ministry but sustains it. Believers are equipped to face any challenge not by their own strength but through the Spirit's power, which prepares and supports them throughout their tasks.
- **Transformation through Submission:** Submitting to God's ways and allowing the Holy Spirit to lead every decision results in a life that genuinely reflects God's power and purpose. This submission is crucial for carrying out the true mission of the Church and living out one's faith authentically.

Conclusion

"Salt and Light" emphasizes the critical role of the Holy Spirit's anointing in empowering believers to live out their faith in ways that visibly demonstrate God's power and love to the world. It challenges Christians to go beyond the walls of the church, carrying the anointing into every area of life, ensuring that their spiritual influence is both seen and felt, thereby glorifying God. The chapter calls for a life of active faith, marked by divine guidance and obedience, making each believer a potent vessel of God's transformative power.

CHAPTER 6

BAPTIZED IN FIRE

Bible Verse

"But you shall receive power when the Holy Spirit has come upon you; and you shall be witnesses to Me in Jerusalem, and in all Judea and Samaria, and to the end of the earth." — Acts 1:8

Introduction

This chapter explores the profound concept of baptism in the Holy Spirit and fire, emphasizing its significance in empowering believers to fulfill their divine purpose and witness for Christ effectively.

Word of Wisdom

"The anointing is necessary for us to go to our world!" James Tan

Main Theme

"Baptized in Fire" delves into the transformative experience of being baptized with the Holy Spirit and fire, highlighting how this spiritual empowerment is crucial for effective ministry and personal growth in God.

Key Points

- Baptism in the Holy Spirit and fire is essential for embarking on effective ministry.
- This baptism signifies complete immersion and transformation by the Spirit's power.
- Jesus instructed His disciples to wait for this baptism before beginning their ministry.
- There are distinct kinds of baptisms mentioned in the scriptures, each with specific purposes.
- Speaking in tongues as a sign of baptism in the Holy Spirit signifies a change in the believer's life direction.
- The baptism in the Holy Spirit equips believers with the power to perform signs and wonders as Jesus did.

Key Themes

- **Concept of Baptism Explained:** The chapter explains baptism as not just a physical immersion but a spiritual

transformation that completely saturates and changes a believer. It highlights the trust required between the one being baptized and the baptizer, emphasizing the depth of surrender to God's process.
- **Distinctive Roles of the Spirit:** It distinguishes between being baptized into the body of Christ, which saves and unites us with other believers, and being baptized with the Holy Spirit, which empowers for service and witness. Both are crucial but serve different divine functions in a Christian's life.
- **Empowerment for Ministry:** The baptism with the Holy Spirit is depicted as essential for ministry, providing the supernatural power needed to carry out God's commands and extend His kingdom on earth.
- **Practical Outcomes of Spiritual Empowerment:** By exploring how the disciples spoke in tongues and performed miracles after their baptism in the Holy Spirit, the chapter underscores the practical, visible outcomes of this spiritual empowerment.
- **Unity and Anointing:** The chapter ties the concept of unity among believers to the flow of anointing, suggesting that harmony in the body of Christ facilitates the movement of the Holy Spirit among His people, leading to greater works and deeper spiritual impact.

Conclusion

"Baptized in Fire" emphasizes the critical role of the Holy Spirit's power in the life of a believer, essential not just for personal sanctification but for effective ministry and the spread of the gospel. The chapter calls believers to seek this baptism actively, to embrace the fullness of their calling, and to engage in their mission with divine power. It reminds us that just as the early disciples needed the Holy Spirit's fire to fulfill their purpose, so do we need this divine empowerment to navigate and impact our world today.

CHAPTER 7

OUR PROGRESSION IN THE ANOINTING

Bible Verse

"Behold, how good and how pleasant it is for brethren to dwell together in unity! It is like the precious oil upon the head, running down on the beard, the beard of Aaron, running down on the edge of his garments." — Psalms 133:1-2

Introduction

This chapter explores the structured and progressive nature of the Holy Spirit's work in believers, highlighting how the anointing flows and develops in a divine order to equip and empower individuals for specific ministries.

Word of Wisdom

"There is order to how the anointing is applied and flows. Like with everything in the universe and in creation, God does

not do anything without order."
James Tan

Main Theme

The chapter discusses the systematic and progressive nature of the anointing, demonstrating how believers can grow in their spiritual abilities through the Holy Spirit's guidance and empowerment.

Key Points

• The Holy Spirit is sent with a specific ministry for specific people, mirroring Jesus' own sent nature.

• The flow of the anointing follows a divine order, starting from the head down, as illustrated by the anointing of Aaron.

• True understanding of the Spirit's work acknowledges both His mysterious ways and the underlying divine order.

• Jesus Himself grew in wisdom and stature, setting an example for believers to progressively grow in their anointing.

• The progression in Jesus' ministry—from turning water into wine to raising Lazarus—illustrates increasing levels of anointing.

Key Themes

- **Divine Order and Sensitivity to the Spirit:** The anointing follows a divine order that mirrors the natural order of the world, emphasizing that while the Spirit's ways can seem mysterious, they are not without structure. This order enables believers to progressively understand and grow more sensitive to the Spirit's guidance.

- **Progressive Growth in Ministry:** The chapter illustrates how Jesus' ministry progressed in complexity and power, serving as a model for believers to aspire to. It suggests that spiritual growth involves moving from simple acts of faith to more profound demonstrations of God's power.
- **Role of Anointing in Empowerment:** Discusses how the anointing serves as empowerment for specific ministries, equipping believers to perform tasks beyond their natural capabilities. This empowerment is crucial for fulfilling the God-given mandates and witnessing effectively.
- **Understanding Signs of the Anointing:** The signs that accompany the anointing, such as healing, speaking in tongues, and casting out demons, are not just random miracles but part of a progressive revelation of the believer's growth in the Spirit.
- **Importance of Unity and Order:** Unity among believers is vital for the anointing to flow effectively. The anointing thrives in environments where believers are united and work together in harmony, as this facilitates a stronger manifestation of God's power.

Conclusion

"Our Progression in the Anointing" underscores the necessity of understanding and cooperating with the Holy Spirit's structured approach to spiritual growth. By following Jesus' example and embracing the divine order of the anointing, believers can advance from basic faith actions to significant spiritual authority and influence, effectively impacting their environments for the Kingdom of God.

CHAPTER 8

REVERENCE AND OBEDIENCE: KEYS TO THE TANGIBLE ANOINTING

Bible Verse

"But solid food belongs to those who are of full age, that is, those who by reason of use have their senses exercised to discern both good and evil." — Hebrews 5:14

Introduction

This chapter delves into the dynamics of growing and training in the anointing, emphasizing the need for believers to engage actively and maturely with the Holy Spirit's manifestations, distinguishing between mere emotional responses and genuine spiritual experiences.

Word of Wisdom

"Yes and no are the two most powerful words in the human vocabulary."
James Tan

Main Theme

The anointing from the Holy Spirit is not random but can be cultivated through training, reverence, and obedience, leading to a tangible and effective ministry.

Key Points

- Training in the anointing is essential for growth and effective ministry.

- Reverence for God's presence and obedience to His directives are crucial.

- Maturity in the spirit involves discerning and acting on God's definitions of good and evil.

- The anointing manifests tangibly and can be felt physically and spiritually.

- Specific incidents of spiritual manifestation require keen sensitivity and proper response.

- The tangible anointing grows stronger through disciplined spiritual training and awareness.

Key Themes

- **Training and Sensitivity:** Mature believers are characterized by their ability to discern spiritually, training their senses to recognize the nuances of the Holy Spirit's guidance. This training involves more than passive reception; it requires active engagement and response to spiritual stimuli.

- **Tangible Manifestation of the Anointing:** The anointing manifests in tangible ways that can be felt physically in the body and seen in the environment, requiring believers to be both sensitive and responsive to these manifestations to effectively minister in the Spirit.
- **Reverence and Obedience:** Reverence for God's presence and obedience to His will are foundational to operating in the anointing. These attitudes ensure that believers respect the sanctity of the anointing and align their actions with divine order.
- **Role of Faith and Discernment:** Faith activates the anointing, drawing out its power to produce visible, tangible results. Believers must exercise discernment to distinguish between true spiritual manifestations and mere emotional reactions.
- **Learning from Biblical Examples:** Biblical figures like Elisha demonstrate the importance of understanding the conditions and contexts in which the anointing operates. Their experiences provide valuable lessons on handling the anointing with respect and wisdom.

Conclusion

"Reverence and Obedience: Keys to the Tangible Anointing" teaches that the anointing is a powerful, tangible force that must be approached with reverence and obedience. By training their senses and cultivating a deep respect for God's presence, believers can grow in their ability to discern and operate in the anointing, leading to effective ministry and spiritual maturity.

CHAPTER 9

JESUS BUILDS HIS CHURCH

Bible Verse

"And I also say to you that you are Peter, and on this rock I will build My church, and the gates of Hades shall not prevail against it." — Matthew 16:18

Introduction

This chapter explores the continuous role of the Holy Spirit in manifesting the ministry of Jesus through His Church, emphasizing the strategic function of the anointing in empowering believers to fulfill God's plans on earth.

Word of Wisdom

"Setting captives free alone does not build the Kingdom; the Kingdom is built when believers are developed and walk in

their callings as ordained by God."
James Tan

Main Theme

The anointing empowers the Church not only to displace darkness but to establish and build God's Kingdom on earth, following Jesus' mission through the five-fold ministry.

Key Points

• The anointing continues Jesus' ministry through the Church, enabling spiritual growth and outreach.

• Believers are empowered to reclaim and transform the earth to reflect God's original intent.

• The anointing establishes righteousness and God's rule, replacing chaotic voids left by dispelled darkness.

• Ministry should focus equally on liberation and spiritual education to prevent recurring spiritual bondage.

• Jesus personified the five-fold ministry roles, which are now distributed among various disciples to build the Church.

• Effective ministry involves both tearing down evil and actively building up the Kingdom with righteousness.

SUMMARY OF RELEASING THE ANOINTING

Key Themes

- **Role of the Anointing in Spiritual Warfare:** The anointing serves a dual purpose: displacing the works of darkness and establishing the Kingdom of God. This process is crucial for maintaining the victories achieved through spiritual warfare, ensuring they lead to lasting transformation and alignment with God's will.
- **Importance of Building After Deliverance:** Simply casting out demons without subsequent spiritual nurturing leads to cycles of bondage; thus, the Church must focus on filling believers with the Word and the Spirit to sustain their freedom and growth.
- **The Five-fold Ministry's Role:** The governance of Jesus over His Church is manifested through the five-fold ministry. These roles, which include apostles, prophets, evangelists, pastors, and teachers, equip the Church to function effectively and mature spiritually.
- **Sustainability in Ministry:** True Kingdom building requires more than initial spiritual victories; it demands ongoing discipleship and development. The Church must engage in continuous teaching and nurturing to foster mature, stable believers who can withstand spiritual challenges.
- **Divine Strategy for Church Expansion:** God's strategy involves using anointed leaders to govern and expand the

Church, ensuring His reign is manifested through transformed lives and communities, which in turn influence broader societal structures.

Conclusion

"Jesus Builds His Church" articulates a vision of the Church not just as a gathering of believers but as a dynamic force equipped with divine anointing to continue Christ's work on earth. Through the systematic application of the anointing and the strategic deployment of the five-fold ministry, the Church is built up, empowered, and mobilized to establish God's Kingdom, ensuring that the light of Christ dispels darkness and transforms societies.

CHAPTER 10

ASSORTED ANOINTINGS ON ASSIGNMENT

Bible Verse

"Till we all come to the unity of the faith and of the knowledge of the Son of God, to a perfect man, to the measure of the stature of the fullness of Christ." — Ephesians 4:13

Introduction

This chapter delves into the dynamic and complementary roles of the five-fold ministry in the Church, likening them to the five fingers on a hand, essential for the Church's full functionality and health.

Word of Wisdom

"All three functions of the anointing have the same Source, flow through the same vessels, and bring us to the same destination." James Tan

Main Theme

The chapter underscores the diversity and interdependence of the five-fold ministry's anointings (apostles, prophets, evangelists, pastors, and teachers), which are crucial for nurturing, governing, and expanding the Church.

Key Points

• Each believer has access to aspects of the five-fold ministry's anointing through the Holy Spirit.

• The five-fold ministry ensures the Church's growth towards unity and Christ-like maturity.

• Each ministry role is distinct yet overlaps with others, facilitating a holistic approach to spiritual leadership.

• Teaching is emphasized as vital across all functions of church life—growing, going, and governing.

• The continuation of these ministries is essential until the Church fully embodies the maturity and unity of Christ.

Key Themes

- **Interdependence of Ministry Roles:**
  The five-fold ministry functions like a team where each role supports and enhances the others. This symbiosis ensures that the Church grows in a balanced and healthy way.

- **Individual and Collective Growth:** While not everyone is called to a specific ministry office, each believer benefits from the anointing present in these roles, contributing to both personal spiritual growth and the collective maturation of the Church.
- **Necessity of Diverse Ministries:** The diversity within the five-fold ministry addresses the various needs of the Church, ensuring that all aspects of church life are nurtured—from doctrine and discipline to outreach and spiritual care.
- **Role of Teaching in the Church:** Teaching is a central function across all the ministries, critical for grounding believers in sound doctrine and equipping them for effective service and witness in the world.
- **Integration of Ministries for Church Health:** The effective functioning of the Church requires the seamless integration of the apostolic, prophetic, evangelistic, pastoral, and teaching ministries, each contributing uniquely to the Church's mission and health.

Conclusion

"Assorted Anointings on Assignment" highlights the critical need for the five-fold ministry within the Church to ensure comprehensive growth and unity. By likening these ministries to the five fingers on a hand, the chapter effectively illustrates how each role is indispensable, working together to fulfill the Church's divine mandate to mirror the fullness and stature of Christ on Earth.

CHAPTER 11

THE FOUNDATION OF THE APOSTLES AND PROPHETS

Bible Verse

"Having been built on the foundation of the apostles and prophets, Jesus Christ Himself being the chief cornerstone." — Ephesians 2:20

Introduction

This chapter explores the foundational roles of apostles and prophets in the Church, emphasizing their historical and ongoing contributions to its structure and spiritual health.

Word of Wisdom

"Prophets see and say. Apostles hear and do. And both are needed to lay the foundations of what God intends for every generation." James Tan

Main Theme

T The chapter articulates the dual role of apostles and prophets as both historical authors of scripture and as contemporary figures who interpret and apply biblical truths, ensuring the Church remains aligned with God's purposes.

Key Points

• Apostles and prophets are foundational to the Church's structure, as authors of the Bible and as continuing guides.

• They do not introduce new revelations but clarify and enforce the existing words of God.

• Their ministries are vital for maintaining doctrinal soundness and strategic spiritual oversight.

• The prophetic ministry includes receiving and declaring new insights into God's will, often through visions.

• Apostles have a unique, broad-reaching ministry that impacts various aspects of Church life.

Key Themes

- **Historical and Contemporary Foundations:** Apostles and prophets laid the historical foundations of the Church through scriptures and continue to guide it today through interpretations that connect past revelations with present circumstances.

- **Role of Continuing Revelation:** While the biblical canon is complete, apostles and prophets today help the Church understand and apply God's word in a relevant way, ensuring the scripture remains a living, active guide.
- **Prophetic Visions and Revelations:** Prophets receive revelations that are not new doctrines but are insights that bring clarity and application to the Church, often involving visions and spiritual discernment that are impactful and directive.
- **Apostolic Leadership and Governance:** Apostles are described as the 'thumb' in the body of Christ, unique in their ability to touch and interact with all other ministry gifts, providing leadership, direction, and foundation for the Church.
- **Interdependence of Ministry Gifts:** The effective functioning of the Church relies on the cooperative and complementary roles of apostles, prophets, and other ministry gifts, each contributing uniquely to the Church's mission and health.

Conclusion

"The Foundation of the Apostles and Prophets" reaffirms the indispensable roles of these ministries in both the historical context and their ongoing necessity in the modern Church. It emphasizes that understanding and embracing these roles allows the Church to remain robust, relevant, and true to its divine calling, all under the chief cornerstone, Jesus Christ.

CHAPTER 12

THE GREATER ANOINTING

Bible Verse
"And do not be drunk with wine, in which is dissipation; but be filled with the Spirit." — Ephesians 5:18

Introduction

This chapter delves into the concept of the corporate anointing within the Church, emphasizing the powerful effects of collective worship and prayer on manifesting God's presence and glory among His people.

Word of Wisdom

"The anointing to gather leads the way to another aspect of the anointing— the corporate anointing." James Tan

Main Theme

The greater anointing is achieved through collective engagement in worship and prayer, magnifying God's presence and allowing His Spirit to move powerfully among His people.

Key Points

• Corporate worship and prayer unleash a greater flow of God's anointing compared to individual efforts.

• True worship involves honoring and exalting God above all, not just emotional stimulation.

• Songs with deep spiritual content have historically facilitated significant spiritual movements and presence.

• Corporate prayer focuses on seeking God's will and magnifying His glory, not just presenting personal requests.

• Historical examples like the dedication of the Temple illustrate the profound impact of God's presence when His people gather in unity.

Key Themes

- **Impact of Unified Worship:** When the Church comes together in true worship, focusing genuinely on God's attributes and deeds, a profound spiritual atmosphere is created that invites the divine presence more powerfully than in isolated worship.
- **Historical Patterns and Modern Worship:** The historical pattern of

worship shows that deeply spiritual songs have always been used to honor God and invoke His presence, contrasting with some modern worship that prioritizes emotional appeal over spiritual depth.

- **Corporate Prayer as Spiritual Governance:** Corporate prayer is a form of spiritual governance, extending God's rule on Earth as the church collectively submits to His will, leading to strategic spiritual insights and directives from the Holy Spirit.
- **Role of Music and Worship Leadership:** Effective worship leaders are crucial in guiding congregations into true spiritual worship rather than mere performances, emphasizing the need for songs that draw participants closer to God and foster an atmosphere conducive to His Spirit.
- **Power of the Corporate Anointing:** The corporate anointing experienced during unified worship and prayer is the pinnacle of spiritual engagement, bringing together the body of Christ in a shared experience of God's power and presence that transcends individual encounters.

Conclusion

"The Greater Anointing" stresses the transformative power of collective worship and prayer, urging the Church to embrace the full scope of its spiritual heritage and contemporary expressions to foster a deeper, more powerful encounter with God. By prioritizing the Spirit over the flesh and unity over individualism, the Church can experience the vastness of God's anointing and presence, leading to profound impacts both internally and in the wider community.

Harrison House is a Spirit-filled, Word of Faith Christian publisher dedicated to spreading the message of faith, hope, and love through our wide range of inspiring publications. Committed to the messages that highlight the power of the Word and Spirit, we provide books, devotionals, and study guides that empower believers to live victorious, faith-filled lives.

Our resources are designed to help readers grow spiritually, strengthen their faith, and experience the transformative power of God's Word. Harrison House is passionate about equipping Christians with the tools they need to fulfill their divine purpose and impact the world for Christ.

www.ingramcontent.com/pod-product-compliance
Lightning Source LLC
LaVergne TN
LVHW051512070426
835507LV00022B/3076